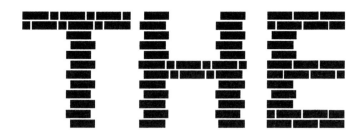

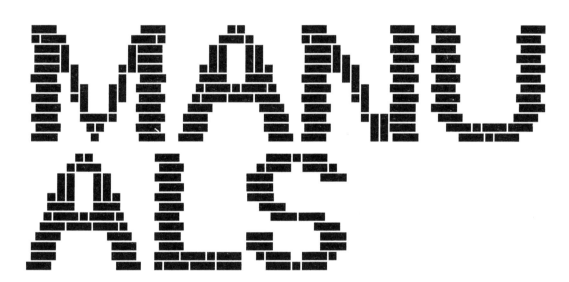

I Positioning of the necessary pipes and installation of the packed-earth foundation.

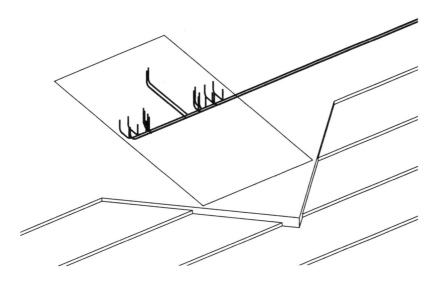

II Construction of the four corner columns in brick.

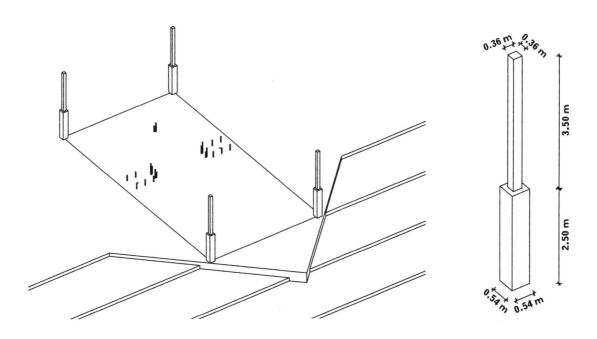

An Architectural Report

El Lokal, Zurich It is quite late in the evening, I am with a friend at El Lokal, and we have left it far too late to have a bite to eat so as to prevent all the white wine from ruining the next day. Whenever I am in the company of Viktor Bänziger, I get lured into countless rounds like this—always another glass—and as a matter of course, I stay for just one more. Viktor is like a stationary magnet, around which the whole bar revolves. The regulars gather around his bar stool and tell crazy stories about the ups and downs of their lives, some of which are barely believable. One of them mined silver in Canada, another is a former professional soccer player, the next is currently taking care of weapon purchases for the Zurich police force. The stories are always fascinating, albeit with an element of repetition if you

are there quite often. Viktor never actually repeats himself though. This evening, he tells of a soccer school that he wants to help build in Madagascar. He says it is complicated. Suddenly, he looks at me with a new thought in his eyes. "Nele, I need an architect!" he says. "Yeah, sure!" I reply. And for the rest of the evening, we say nothing more about it: It is a done deal.   The next day, I receive an email with some plans and photos of the property that he has already bought for his local contact in Madagascar, Titus Solohery Andriamananjara. I have a hard time understanding the documentation. It is like a huge ball of string that cannot be unraveled. I am unable to figure out where the property is even located, which documents are from the local Madagascans, and which sketches are from Viktor's colleagues. This is because Titus has already sent Viktor some plans as a suggestion on how to construct the soccer field and

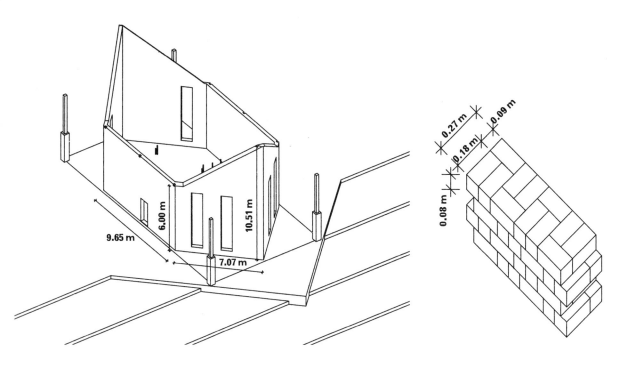

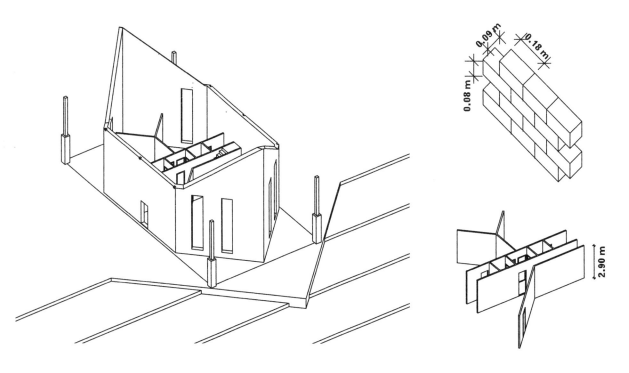

school, but they are cryptic. There is a small soccer field with a really wide border, plus way too many buildings—a whole village of them, in fact—whose layouts do not always add up. I spend some time trying to understand how people are supposed to get past the stairs and reach the toilets, until I decide that there really must be a mistake in the planning. After having bought the land, El Lokal cannot make any further money transfers without understanding what is being built where. Somehow, it all has to be untangled.   Human intelligence is evenly distributed around the globe. Within Madagascar's relatively isolated natural cycle, people have developed ways of living and building that work for their island. But as Viktor and the whole team at El Lokal are financing the project, perhaps a misleading process is going on in the minds of the local village community and they are developing unfulfillable expectations. Or maybe their way of talking about and depicting buildings is just too far removed from ours. To me, this collaboration comes across as an unsolvable puzzle. That gives me an idea: instead of floor plans, I will draw axonometrics—a means of representation not used in Europe for construction but for instructions, for example, on how to make model airplanes. Such model airplanes are quite complex objects, but thanks to the step-by-step instructions anyone can assemble them. I believe this mode of representation has the magic of a universal language that makes implementation possible across continents and cultures. Sitting down to write this text today, I think about how right I actually was—and wrong at the same time, unfortunately. As an architect, I can solve architectural issues, but there is more to the world than just architecture.   Viktor and I decide to build the small building for the groundskeeper first.

V   Flooring on the second floor.

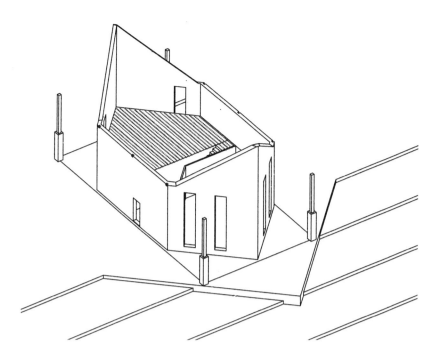

VI   Half-brick-thick interior masonry on the second floor.

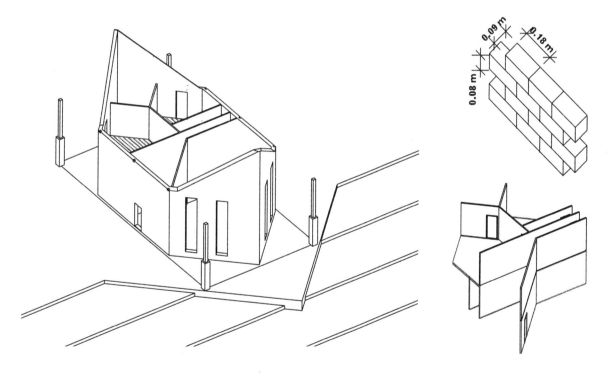

Titus explains to us that the groundskeeper is very important for guarding the property and needs his own building. We consider this a test run, to see whether collaborating like this on opposite sides of the globe can work. We send him the implementation plans in the post, printed and signed by us, while Dottore, one of Viktor's colleagues at El Lokal, sends money via Western Union to buy the bricks for the whole project. In multiple emails, Titus explains to us that it is now already very important to buy bricks for the second and much bigger building. An instinctive mistrust awakens within me. It is still not even clear to me whether the property really exists. The photos of the purchase contract and hill could have just been thrown together somehow. I suggest that he email us photos of the purchased bricks and of them being transported to the site, so we can get confirmation that the transferred money is being used properly. In response, we receive blurry pixelated photos of a pile of bricks. The pictures look like internet photos from the 1990s. Fortunately, Titus sends photos with better focus a week later—some of what Dottore transferred may have gone toward the purchase of a digital camera—and the same pile of bricks can now be seen on a hill. I compare it with the very first photos of the purchased property. The topography is the same. I am somewhat reassured, and ashamed of my mistrust. From then on, photos of the progressing construction work come regularly. I love every single one of these pictures. The camera creates a mysterious blurry edge and only shows parts of the image in focus, much like an analog camera. Some of the pictures look to me like oil paintings by a contemporary artist.

VII   Ceiling on the second floor.

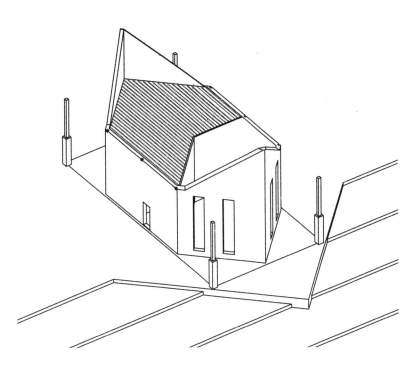

VIII   Roof beams on top of the masonry.

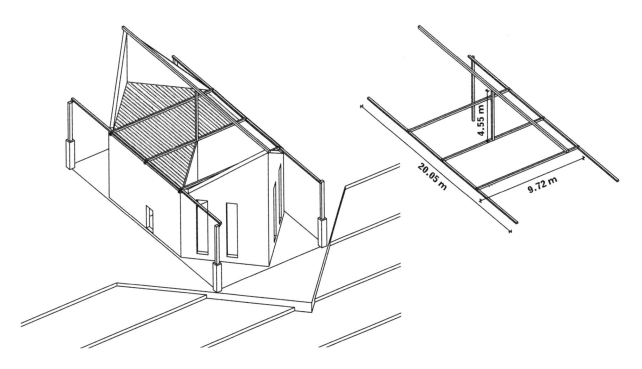

4.55 m
20.05 m
9.72 m

Johannesburg, South Africa   Together with three colleagues, I am in Johannes-
burg, conducting research into skyscrapers and their
changing use over time. My geographical location
means this is my only opportunity to visit the Advan FC
project's construction site. From Zurich the journey
would have cost as much as a whole house in Madagascar, but here in Johannesburg the island is just
around the corner. I am nervous. I have booked the flight
ticket, but shortly before departure I read in a German-
language online newspaper that the plague, the horror
of the Middle Ages, still exists in Madagascar—in one
specific rural region. Just like long ago, the inhabitants
there fall ill with the Black Death, developing large
black lumps, which then burst inwardly and lead to
death. I google the region. With surprise and horror, I
find that I will be traveling to the very same place. The

book *Narcissus and Goldmund* by Hermann Hesse has
cemented my mental picture of the plague as a biblical,
irreversible, and deeply evil disease. For a moment, I actually consider somehow getting out of taking the flight.

Antananarivo, Madagascar   Titus Solohery Andriamananjara picks me up at the
airport. He comes in his Peugeot, which I recognize from
the first construction-site photos. He is a quiet man. I
think he is waiting to see what to expect from me. We
speak in French and luckily, after a long monosyllabic
drive, we do find a topic that we can both relate to: he
raves about Viktor. He tells me that, when visiting a
market in Antananarivo, Viktor bought so much Madagascan music that he was almost unable to carry it all
and kept dropping CDs. Titus found this very funny and
it made an impression on him. I suppose this is because

IX   Walls leading up to the roof.

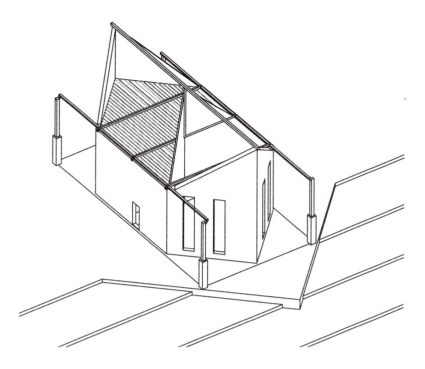

X   Support structure, roof beams.

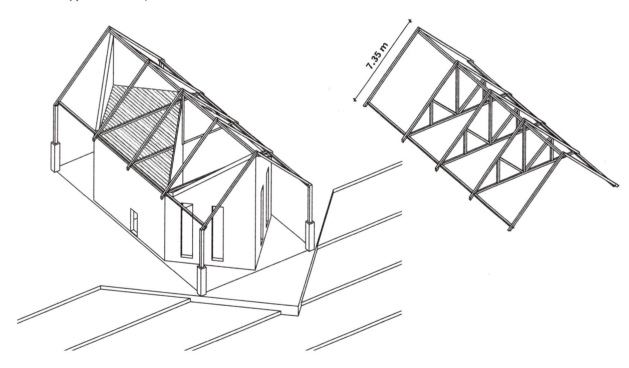

7.35 m

of Victor's great interest in the local music, and his grim determination to explore it thoroughly. From now on, the atmosphere between us is fine. On the following day, we drive to the construction site. It is a long trip even though the highlands are not so many kilometers away, as the roads are in such poor condition that it takes us many hours. Built fewer than ten years ago by Chinese companies, the roads have become an impossible problem for drivers. All that is left of them are asphalt islands between stretches of hilly earth and large protrusions of rock. Titus drives his Peugeot very slowly over the big rocks. I take note of his driving style. Since then, I have been able to get over any terrain, no matter how rough, in any car.   On the building site, the building for the groundskeeper is now standing. All the construction workers come inside it with me, and we are all proud of having realized it so well. However, Titus explains to

me that this building would be better for him, as a kind of clubhouse, and the groundskeeper actually needs a smaller one.   We now want to start on the large building: a place in which to teach, eat, and even spend the night. With the builder, we determine the position of the main building and discuss the plans I have brought with me. They have also started digging the soccer field out of the hill already. For this, they are using an archaic but clever technique: holes are made in the slope with the aid of shovels, then the undermined sections are broken away from the terrain. When it comes to the soccer field, we have our first differences of opinion. Titus considers it very important that we adhere to the dimensions of international soccer fields, meaning the big stadiums where the World Cup is played. Viktor and I try to counter this as we think a smaller field will do, out here in the sparsely populated highlands. Looking

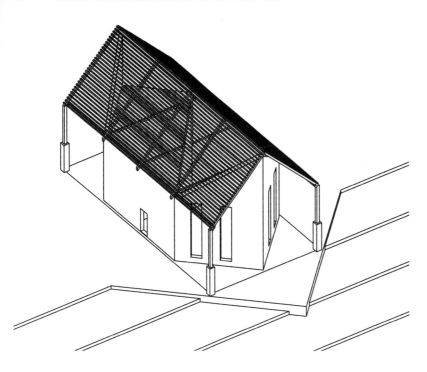

XII   Covering the roof with tiles.

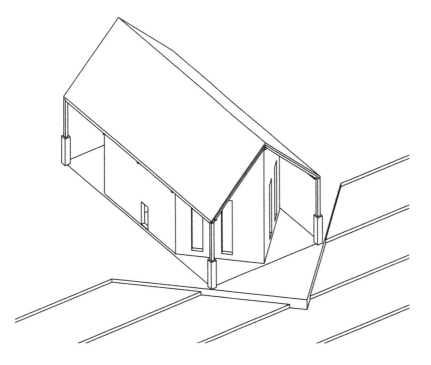

back, I almost have the feeling that our resistance was what prompted Titus to get the largest ever soccer field leveled out.   During my stay, Titus also shows me a national park, where I see lemurs—those primates that move lithely like cats and exist naturally only in Madagascar. Magical creatures, somehow. I am reminded of the lemurs in Masoala Hall, a rainforest zoo in Zurich: their intelligence had been underestimated by the zookeepers, who eventually discovered that they had long been secretly activating the photoelectric sensor to enter an adjacent store at night. This was only noticed because one lemur fell asleep among the stuffed animals and frightened an employee by jumping out of the display when she arrived in the morning.   The construction work is progressing, the school is being built, and I am enjoying making discoveries about the local construction methods. In Madagascar, bricks are fired

locally and produced in every second highland village. The locals take the earth they live on and shape it into bricks. The air-dried bricks are then assembled in pyramidal sculptures with a cavity at the bottom, via which the entire pile is fired. These large stacks of bricks with clouds of smoke escaping from the sides are to be found all along the roads in Madagascar. Although they are just part of a production process, they are among the most poetic architectural entities I have seen. I am learning all the time, marveling at the different approach to construction. The locals make the scaffolding for the school out of wooden sticks, inserted in gaps in the brick wall. It is an interweaving of scaffolding and building, which gives rise to a temporary all-encompassing artwork. I like the pink colors used all over the highlands and am amazed by the simple process with which the property's trees are turned into the roof structure's wooden beams.

XIII   Installation of doors and windows.

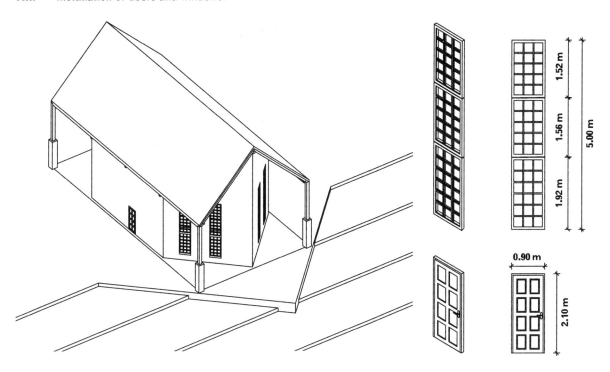

XIV   Addition of necessary sinks, toilets, and showers.

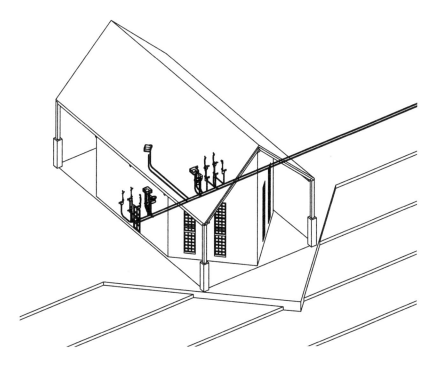

Zurich, Switzerland   We provide volumetric instructions, they provide self-directed implementation of these in the construction process and in the details. At the same time, unfortunately, the ruptures between Zurich and Antananarivo become more and more pronounced. Titus insists that they have to build a fence around the property because otherwise the zebus would eat the grass on the soccer field, but Viktor thinks this is precisely how the soccer field should be run. A real dispute breaks out. The emails from Madagascar come with many consecutive exclamation marks and question marks. In my mind, the word "zebu" has had several exclamation marks behind it ever since. At some point, Titus shuts off completely. He really insists on this fence. Viktor gives in, Dottore transfers the necessary money, and I make a sketch of how the fence should be built. But it never does get built and

I am still wondering what they did with that money. The requests for money transfers keep coming in anyway. The mayor gives Titus a hefty fine because excavated earth from the soccer field falls on the public road during removal. At one point, there is an accident on the building site: a construction worker falls down the newly installed well and only barely survives. On another occasion, Titus has a seriously ill grandchild and asks for help. Are we being told the truth or not? Where do you draw the line between cooperation and aid? It is difficult to access the situation clearly. Even the attached photos are not always very conclusive. After protracted attempts to once again limit the support to just the construction project itself, which has actually been finished in the meantime, Viktor breaks off contact. The school and grounds remain as a gift to Titus, who now does with them whatever he wants.   Did we fail, or did

Floor plan, first floor

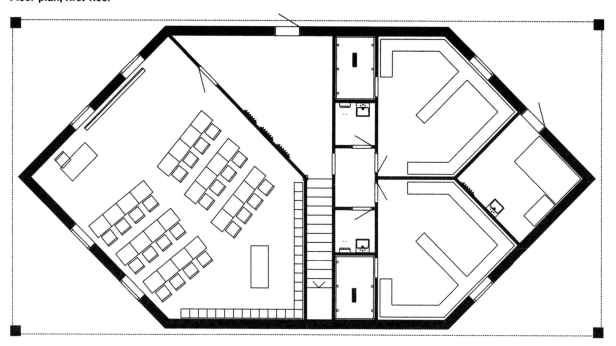

Floor plan, second floor

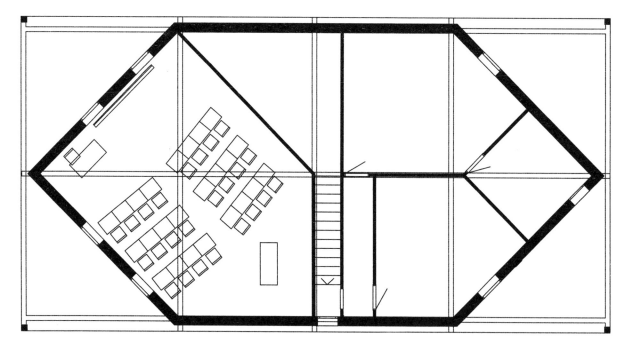

we realize a great project? I think both are true. The whole collaboration was based on mutual trust and Titus is a very serious, decent man. However, although it is a very modest project, Titus's connection to far-off Switzerland possibly raised expectations too high. I assume the community were demanding that Titus share more and more of his presumed access to foreign wealth with everyone. Their notion of this source's vastness probably grew to fantastical proportions over time, simply because it would be so terrific if it actually existed. Recently, a story in the newspaper reminded me of how our project went. The soccer player Lionel Messi saw a photo of a young boy in Afghanistan wearing a Messi T-shirt that had been made by hand out of plastic bags. This moved the sportsman and he arranged for a shirt that he signed to be sent to the boy. The neighbors in the village then thought his family were friends with the world-famous

Messi and they all wanted a share of the vast sums of money that the family were now surely receiving. In the end, the whole family had to flee the village because the pressure had become so great. As for our project, I hope the Advan FC site is now a place where soccer is played, lessons are taught, and meals are shared. And the thought that zebus can graze there too makes me happy.

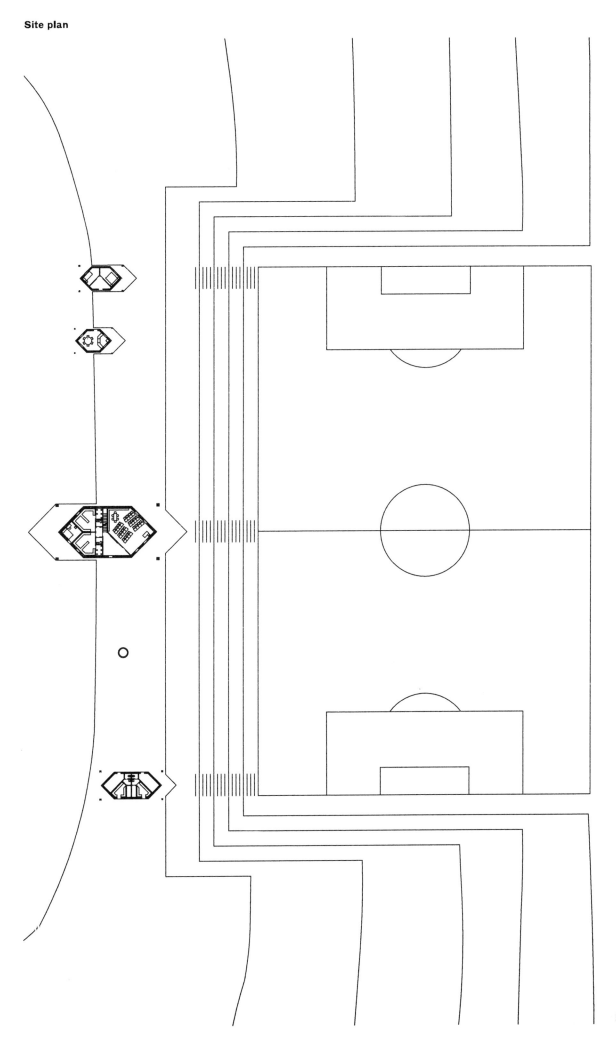

Cutting Corners   Tom Emerson

A photograph shows two men holding spade-like tools, with a sharp cutting edge against a red-earth escarpment; one is raising his tool into the air preparing for a thrust downwards while the other is at the bottom of his swing, the blade two feet below the ground. They belong to a broad category of earth-cutting and -moving tools found all over the world. But these are specific. The steel end is flatter than a spade or shovel, ending in a slightly curved cutting blade. In fact, they appear almost more like oversized chisels made for carving rather than digging producing a sharp vertical face of deep-red clay below a fringe of meadow. It is work in progress; at the base, a series of new horizontal incisions about fifty centimetres in height and two metres in length cut at forty-five degrees into the dry clay suggest that there are more earth works to come. The action of earth cutting seems as natural to the place as the hammering is to the North American carpenter or stone-cutting to the Italian mason—a culture of making and of work tied to the geology and the territory. Between the two men, above the red escarpment, a prow of brickwork divides the sky as if it were cut from the chisel at work below. It is the leading corner of a new building, a clubhouse and community hall for a football field being carved and levelled from the gently sloping landscape. The image contains the whole project: past, present and future.

The process of landworks and building appear as one. Forms carved in the ground echo the form built above them. Of course, soon after this picture is taken the football field will be flat and the escarpment will be neatly terraced up to the building. But the building will retain a powerful echo of previous events and signifies the arrival of the beautiful game.

The figures in the landscape are part of a series of precisely and practically honed architectural operations. The Centre d'Education FC Advan comprises three buildings and a fresh-water well set around a football field that forms a great landscape structure. Hosting the local football team and schoolchildren, the place is a community space for sports and education in Ambanja, northern Madagascar. The project was initiated and funded by Viktor Bänziger, the owner of El Lokal cultural bar in Zurich, who, seduced by the music and musicians from Madagascar performing in his venue set off on a journey to discover the country. And since his love for music is matched by his love of football, his journey to Madagascar led to his supporting the creation of a place for sport and education. *

* The story that led to these projects is wonderfully recounted by Bänziger
in „The Wonderful Moments Outweigh the Rest"

Terrain and buildings were worked on by hand with simple tools.

The Centre d'Education FC Advan is literally made from the ground on which it stands, but it is also an exchange between continents. Successful building projects often involve a combination of sustained purpose to achieve a goal with coincidence that turns effort into opportunity. When Bänziger needed someone to design the buildings, he knew not only an architect with a kindred spirit for the social aims of the project but also one of the rare contemporary practitioners with a profound understanding of brick. Several years before, during her architectural studies at ETH Zurich, Nele Dechmann had undertaken research on the relatively unknown monolithic brick Church of St Bride (Gillespie, Kidd & Coia, East Kilbride, Scotland, 1957). Heavy, earthy, with very occasional delicate turns—here was an architecture as ancient as it was modern, as formally abstract as it was pragmatic. And the study of this forgotten corner of architectural history was, for Dechmann, the beginning of an architectural journey into the contemporary use of traditional materials. She replayed it in her wonderful library in Köpenick, Berlin (2008), which reinterpreted the deep brick diaphragm walls for circulation and small chambers around the main halls.

Köpenick Library, Berlin

So it was only natural that the red clay that defines the landscape and traditional brick architecture of the northern highlands of Madagascar would be the means and ends of the community buildings for the football club. Images from the site and surrounding villages are marked by vivid red-clay paths that draw lines across the landscape and in the simple rectangular volumes of local buildings. Once fired, the red clay emerges lighter but its deep colour often returns when the houses are rendered in unfired clay. The actions of cutting, digging, forming and firing clay are fundamental to any architectural culture able to transform its ground into structure and space, yet an architectural language always bears unique characteristics of scale, bond and texture. Scale is closely tied to the body and the hand. Each brick is stacked according to bond patterns for strength and/or sculptural effect. Material and structural efficiency has brought brick into partnership with structural framing—usually, but not always, in reinforced concrete. But brickwork cannot be understood as purely image. Dechmann started with her own visit to Madagascar, studying not only the buildings but the entire process from earth to house, from geology to community.

St Bride Cathedral, East Killbride, Scottland

The three buildings reflect much of what she experienced and documented on site. They bear a strong relationship to the village architecture but they are also other. The traditions, economies and technologies that determine architectural design are all at play but transformed just enough for a slight abstraction to turn building into a new architecture. Aligned with the pitch's centre line, the largest of the three buildings containing the clubhouse/classroom. Rectangular plan under a timber pitched roof, its four corners are cut off at forty-five degrees leaving the roof oversailing. In one simple operation, the local type reveals a series of spatial and formal inventions without rhetoric or unnecessary expense. For the users, it creates four external spaces sheltered from the blistering sun adjacent to the double-height hall overlooking the pitch. The plan playfully embodies the right angles and forty-five degrees without discomfort. In the landscape, a new form emerges from familiar origins. Cutting the corners creates a striking vertical line up the centre, extending the tallest dimension of the building to the apex of the roof. The leading edge divides the sunlight into even finer geometries of brightness and shade. It is as if the half-way line of the football pitch has been extended right up to the heavens—the symmetry of the game raised into architecture.

The free overhanging corners of the roof are propped by tall brick columns; stout at the base and as they rise to pick up the load. This is a pragmatic and efficient use of material but also a matter of form and lightness. Terracotta tiles with half-round ends, also made from the red clay, cover the two primary buildings; the third is thatched. The process and project are full of space and form, but not in some aloof manner of distant theory or rhetoric but as the product of human action and exchange: action on the part of the architect that gives agency to all the physical and organisational processes by people on the ground. The whole project was described by the architect as an assembly of simple parts between Zurich and Ambanja, carefully and concisely laid out in three-dimensional line drawings like those for a model aeroplane. Starting with the single unit of brick, the bonding patterns are arranged and geometries clearly laid out with small details providing accents for significant moments.

From afar, the buildings have something of the temple about them. Familiar but strange, perhaps like the monumentality of the brick kilns that Dechmann documented? No, lighter: more like the abstract geometry of a football pitch, used in the same way all over the world yet leaving no two games alike. Close up, a more tactile dimension is revealed. Two modest areas of brickwork laid obliquely produce a field of small shadows around the entrance, recalling the brick corbels over the entrance of St Brides—small gestures where the makers will meet the users animate by creating a pattern of light and shadow. And to finish it all, the exposed concrete frame—painted in the same pink as the window frames—blends contrasting materials while adding a touch of millennial style.

The men have finished their work. The tools have been put away. The pitch is level and neatly terraced up to the slope. The buildings stand in material union with the ground, geometry aligned with the game. Boys and girls, in vertically striped blue-and-yellow kit marked "El Lokal," take the crucial corner.

When a vacation trip develops into an architectural project: Zurich's award-winning cultural-bar owner Viktor Bänziger describes how his activity in Madagascar came about—and how it makes him happy, despite it not being entirely successful. A story of joy and suffering on a troubled island.

"The nature, the animals, and especially the music were what I and my partner Johanna, as an island lover, found particularly appealing about Madagascar. In the bar El Lokal, which I opened in Zurich over twenty years ago—as well as in its predecessor, El Internacional—bands from Madagascar performed frequently. They would tell me about their homeland: about beautiful spots but also about numerous shady aspects, all somehow interconnected, such as poverty, decaying infrastructure, corruption, and violent conflicts. As a result, we started to get interested in a corner of the world that, despite our many travels, we knew little about—even though it is the second-largest island state after Indonesia! We decided to see it for ourselves. So at the end of 2014, we set off, with a great deal of curiosity, to a country whose descriptions made it sound simultaneously fascinating and forbidding.

Charm in adversity

I was prepared for many things, but I must confess: Madagascar confronted me with a world that I had not come close to experiencing anywhere else. This experience already began at the airport in the capital, Antananarivo, which appeared to be deserted. There was nobody to help you find your way around. That irritated even me, a seasoned traveler.

As if that were not bad enough, my luggage had failed to arrive. That happens to me quite often—but here there was an apparent system behind the absence, as I soon learned: Although the airline we had chosen lands only once a week in Antananarivo, a local advised me to visit the baggage counter again the very next day, which I did. And suddenly, there it was: my bag. I was only allowed to redeem it after paying a considerable storage fee though. Having barely arrived in the country, I had already been introduced to the aforementioned corruption, which is simply rife in its poverty-stricken areas.

The food markets give a clear indication of how precarious the situation is in Madagascar with regard to both health and the economy. You cannot see what is on display there as it is encased in black swarms of flies! At the same time, the people have to be grateful if there are enough products to meet their daily needs at all. Many suffer from hunger. And they live in undignified conditions—forced to relieve themselves in rivers, for example.

In addition, there are political injustices. The country is a republic but with authoritarian characteristics. Violations of human rights, enrichment at the expense of the population, presidential coups, and so on and so forth are all to be found there.

Despite all the deterrents, Madagascar does exhibit a peculiar charm. In general, there is something double-edged about the country: the good and the bad are close companions, and sometimes mutually dependent. At least, that is how it seems to me.

Luxury and holes, lives and corpses

As a tourist, you get warned about criminal attacks, for example. We took this seriously, but nevertheless strolled down the alleys—albeit carefully—and remained unmolested. This journey of discovery led us to a shopping center. I was shocked by the sight of it: it was all so pompous and luxurious that it came across as really obscene. However, if you go to the rear of the building and through the door, you are catapulted back into squalor. A train station stands there, or what is left of it. Where the tracks should be, there are gaping holes. No train has arrived there for a long time.

This recurring ambivalence of Madagascar brings me to the encounter from which the architectural project arose. As the railroad lines were missing or no longer in existence, Johanna and I realized that we would have to use another means of transport to explore the country. One option was to use the public minibuses. However, these discarded vehicles from Europe are in a pitiful condition, often do not even have windows, and are used for all kinds of cargo. We once even observed a man carrying a sack that contained a corpse.

It takes time to get used to such passengers, and we wanted to avoid them. That is why we chose a private taxi. We took it from Antananarivo, in the country's interior, to the east: toward Sainte Marie, an island just off the coast. Although there were only a few hundred kilometers between our starting point and the ferry landing, the trip took several days. The roads are full of potholes. To survive them unscathed, you can often only allow yourself to drive at walking pace. You cannot help but wonder about the various

Chinese construction companies that have a presence there. Each of them has been awarded large contracts to improve the road network, due to a lack of local know-how. So are corners being cut? Is money that is designated for materials being misappropriated? Or are the locals not taking enough care of the infrastructure? I suspect a combination of all the above.

Reasonable scale, but unimagined dimensions

Fortunately, our cab driver turned out to be a gifted storyteller. We talked with him for hours. Thanks to Titus Solohery Andriamananjara, we found it an entertaining journey. And little by little, we developed a better understanding of how Madagascar works—and of how it simply does not. Over the course of our conversations, familiarity increased, and Titus, as we were allowed to call him, mentioned being president of a soccer club for children and youths. As a former young player myself, who had gone through all the junior levels in Switzerland, I was particularly pleased about this—even more so when he explained that he accepted not only boys but also girls, and that he made sure they all went to school.

The project demanded a great deal of effort from everyone involved, but was run on a voluntary basis. I immediately decided to support it. For me, it was not about the sport—it could equally have been music lessons, for example, that Titus was involved in—the main thing was that children were benefitting!

As the municipalities do not usually install soccer fields, the few that exist are widely scattered over various privately owned plots of land. The kids had to be prepared to walk long distances. To make matters worse, Titus was unable to permanently rent a field. In order to end his constant search for training grounds, I offered him the money to buy his own. It would take about 6,000 Swiss francs, he told me, as he showed us a field with a basic dressing room on the way.

In his home village, situated in an extremely poor area near Antananarivo, he eventually found a suitable piece of land. As far as I understood, a relative owned it. The aim was to flatten the terrain and add a container as a changing room. A project on that scale seemed reasonable to me. As a foreigner, I felt that it came across as neither too petty nor too patronizing.

However, I had underestimated the dynamics that such a project could trigger in a country like Madagascar. It all quickly took on unimagined dimensions. Everything became more expensive and complicated. There it is again, that ambivalence: the positive and the negative go hand in hand!

National style—international recipe

Shortly after our return to Switzerland, I received the first plans. They had obvious flaws though. The pixelated graphics looked as if they had come from an old computer game. The field was embedded in surroundings that did not correspond to the real conditions but to some fantasy, with streets and houses that simply did not exist. On top of that, the ratios of scale—for instance, between the border and the actual playing field—were not right at all. And in the building, a staircase was placed in such a way that it blocked the entrance to the showers.

Despite the errors, Titus wanted funding for what was depicted. This made it clear to me that I had to bring in a professional. I contacted Nele Dechmann. She had worked in our previous bar, El Internacional, during her studies and had since become a qualified architect.

To my delight, Nele immediately agreed to assist me. An exchange ensued that ushered in the most gratifying phase of the project. We pressed ahead with it together and decided to expand the envisaged changing-room facilities into a meeting place with a school.

Nele responded to the locals' odd designs cautiously, respectfully—and creatively. She developed universally understandable assembly instructions to help them do the work themselves. These led to the goal step by step, like when assembling an Ikea cabinet. This apportioning also allowed us to provide the funding in installments. We only wanted to transfer money after the completion of each agreed step.

The privileged underprivileged

Nele considered it important to avoid imposing a Western style on the new plans. Instead, she oriented herself toward the local architecture. The only type of building found in the region has two floors, made from hand-fired bricks, and a wooden roof. She supplemented this traditional structure with an element of her own: angled corners at each end, to provide shade!

In order to get an overview, Nele went on a trip to Madagascar herself. She liked what she saw. The workers were putting in a lot of effort and making good progress. However, she also noted that Titus and his colleagues wanted to supplement the central building with two smaller ones—one on either side. She was unable to find out the exact reasons. It was said, for instance, that one of the buildings should be made available to the groundskeeper. During discussions, on the other hand, it then emerged that this would exaggerate the latter's status and that Titus, as president, could instead take one for himself. Last but not least, there was the mayor, who surely also had ideas about how the property should be used.

Back in Zurich, Nele consulted me. It seemed to us as though the entire village community was now expressing its desires. This impression was intensified by emails from Titus, in which he kept formulating new aspirations. We knew that the plague had broken out again in the area, which of course complicated everything. But suddenly a fence was required to protect the field from grazing cattle, then a new roof after a storm, then an access road for the bus. From afar, it was difficult for us to judge which measures were justified. What was easy to determine though, was that the associated requests for money would never end.

To a certain extent, I can understand such behavior. It is only human nature, given the poverty that prevails in Madagascar. Titus was undoubtedly put under immense pressure—and was now considered privileged himself because he had met me, a foreigner who had to be considered downright rich compared with the local population. Absolutely everyone expected him to hand them some of the money that was coming in. There would have been consequences if he had refused. That was something that he, as a taxi driver in a small village community, could not afford to do.

I never felt that I had been deceived by a con man. Moreover, I firmly believe that you should give something back in life—all the more so if you live in wealthy Switzerland. So I have no desire to condemn Titus. But my willingness to help should not be confused with naivety.

Happiness—despite all the suffering

The cost of the entire project ultimately rose to around 110,000 Swiss francs. That was far beyond the envisaged scope. I made several attempts to explain my position to Titus. Without success. Instead of accepting compromises, he lost all sense of proportion. The mutual trust was gone. With a heavy heart, I brought things to an end. I had become aware that, due to social pressures, the project would never be finished. It would only have kept entailing more payments.

Nevertheless, it is important for me to emphasize the fact that the wonderful moments outweigh the rest—in Zurich, as well as in Madagascar. It was El Lokal, for instance, that made the project possible in the first place. The entire amount that went to Titus came from this bar. My crew backed the idea from the very start. Not only did they approve of us spending working capital on it but, in the meantime, they also waived a wage increase. At the same time, our guests accepted a temporary surcharge on the price of beer to generate a contribution toward the buildings.

I remember numerous gestures like that, both large and small. For example, when Johanna invited guests to celebrate her fiftieth birthday at El Lokal, she did not want any gifts. Instead, well-wishers were asked to donate to the project in Madagascar. They all did so, without hesitation. On another occasion, in an equally uncomplicated manner, we were allowed to use a sum that had been raised for a book via crowdfunding but was no longer needed because the publication failed to materialize.

Such solidarity is extraordinary—and a distinguishing feature of El Lokal. Many colleagues have been with us for years, even decades. This has led to a nice situation in which some of them have members of their families' next generation, or even the generation after that, working with us.

Young people are often on our team anyway, like Nele once was. They study at university, for instance, and pay their way by working part-time. A few of these were keen on going to Madagascar for a while, on an exchange visit that would have seen us invite their Madagascan peers for a stay in Zurich. My daughter Nayah was doing a lot to help make this intercultural exchange happen. But before it could take concrete shape, it was abruptly halted—by an insidious illness that took her life far too soon.

Consistency after the break-off

I am now closing the Madagascar chapter—but certainly still have a soft spot for the local kids. I will never forget them chasing the ball, wearing the shirts that we arranged to be made for them. I accept that they only received half of the material sent, as the rest probably fell victim to corruption. That is part of my double-edged experience with that country. Like my relationship with Titus.

We are not in touch at all anymore. But although our friendship is broken and the project probably ended long ago, I would not want to have missed out on any of those experiences—not despite but because of the associated ambivalence. After all, that is what makes life so very fascinating!

(This text is based on an interview the author conducted with Viktor Bänziger in the summer of 2020)

When Viktor Bänziger (b. 1952) tackles a project, he does so with body and soul, heart and mind. He dislikes half measures. His Zurich cultural bar El Lokal—the popular, self-proclaimed "very last island on the Sihl"—bears witness to this. Ever since it opened on August 1, 2000, it has offered a carefully curated range of small but select concerts featuring bands of all kinds from all over the world.

They get an opportunity to play in front of a wondrous backdrop. Thanks to travel companions who have ventured far and wide, El Lokal's rooms are filled with countless mementos—ranging from electric guitars and Dadaist-looking artworks to a sneering skeleton on the ceiling. In addition, paintings by known and unknown artists, photographs, illustrations, postcards, and newspaper clippings adorn the walls—so Marlon Brando, for example, is just as likely to be found gazing down at the hustle and bustle as Frida Kahlo or Diego Armando Maradona. In 2011, the City of Zurich honored this distinctive form of cultural mediation with a lifetime achievement award, for a wealth of accomplishments.

Viktor Bänziger completed a commercial apprenticeship at the former banking association Bankverein; as a soccer player, he almost made it into the first team at Zurich's Grasshopper Club (a club, incidentally, that he does not like that much); he founded the music store Jamarico; he became a culture journalist and finally a bar owner, who has turned his profession into a calling.

His projects in Zurich are locally based but globally influenced—they ease the travel bug and yet they mean home. The diverse crowd that they attract encounters a patron who, to this day, refuses to let himself be deprived of personally caring for his guests' well-being on a daily basis, even under conditions complicated massively by the coronavirus.

Viktor Bänziger is full of empathy and generosity: a convinced philanthropist—as shown to no small extent by his activity in Madagascar. That is where he sent the prize money he received from the city: all 15,000 Swiss francs. For him, anything else would have been out of the question. (by Silvan Lerch)

Tom Emerson cofounded 6a architects in London in 2001 producing buildings and landscapes for the arts and education. Alongside practice, he is dean of the Department of Architecture, ETH Zurich and professor of architecture, where he leads a studio exploring the relationship between making, landscape, and ecology. Books include *Never Modern* (2014), *6a architects 2010–17* (El Croquis, 2018) and a series of *Atlases* on *Forst* (2012), *Galway* (2013), *Glasgow* (2016), and *Pachacamac*, Peru (2021).

Silvan Lerch shares Viktor Bänziger's passion for culture and soccer. Like the man he has portrayed here, he is involved in cultural mediation himself: as a journalist for SRF (Schweizerische Radio- und Fernsehgesellschaft —the Swiss Broadcasting Corporation) and for soccer-culture magazine ZWÖLF; and also as a freelance (book) author, filmmaker, and exhibition organizer. He holds a doctorate in German philology and is active as an amateur historian—for instance, at the FCZ-Museum Zurich (so he supports not the club that Viktor Bänziger played for but its archrival). This love was kindled in 1980 during the "Zurich is burning" protests, a movement he kept on his mind until today, in his mid-forties—as documented by several multimedia projects on the history of his native city. He enjoys traveling the world but favors one destination in particular: the "very last island on the Sihl."

Editors	Nele Dechmann, Atlas Studio
Texts	Nele Dechmann, Tom Emerson, Silvan Lerch
Translations	Simon Thomas
Copy editing	Ian McDonald
Proofreading	Colette Forder
Photography	Titus Solohery Andriamananjara, Nele Dechmann
Plans	Nele Dechmann
Design	Atlas Studio
Image editing	Herr & Frau Rio (Riso), Marjeta Morinc (Offset)
Printing	Herr & Frau Rio (Riso), F & W Druckcenter (Offset)
Binding	F & W Druckcenter

© 2022 Park Books AG, Zurich
© for the texts: the authors
© for the images: the artists

Park Books
Niederdorfstrasse 54
8001 Zurich
Switzerland
www.park-books.com

Park Books is being supported by the Federal Office of Culture with a general subsidy for the years 2021–2024.

ISBN 978-3-03860-269-9